# Startup Essentials

## *The Simple, Step-by-Step Guide to Successfully Start Your Own Business*

### By Rachael L. Thompson

D1373231

# Introduction

This book explains the basics of starting any business in easy-to-understand language. With the use of examples and simple breakdown of concepts you will gain an understanding and confidence to begin to take the next steps in your business. Perhaps you have a great idea already or are just exploring what it would be like to start your own business. This book will help you become clear on all start-up options. This is not meant for those with extensive business knowledge; it is meant for the average person who is looking for more out of life but does not yet have the skills or information to turn their ideas into a successful business.

You will learn the nuts and bolts of starting a business, how to figure out if your idea will be successful, decide the best way to run your business, as well as marketing and branding information that many beginning business books leave out, but are essential to the long term success of all start-ups. In addition, you will find links to credible, completely free online resources (not affiliated with this book) to help you as you plan for your business. This book will educate and encourage without overwhelming you.

There are far too many people with great ideas who never pursue them, with underutilized skills, and with amazing gifts that the world never gets to see because they do not take the next step in starting their business. There are also far too many start-up failures because people jump in without proper preparation. This book will help prevent you from falling into any of those categories.

# Table of Contents

# Chapter 1

## Developing Your Million Dollar Idea

Every business starts exactly the same, with an idea. If you do not have an idea or if you have a general idea but are not clear about specifics, it is a great time to brainstorm. This book will not only help you understand how to start a business but can also help you develop and clarify your concept.

If you have no idea where to start, simply begin to think of what interests you. Is there something that you are very knowledgeable about or something that people are always asking you to help with? Write down everything that you can think of, even if it initially seems silly or impossible. Next, write down your strengths and weaknesses. Be blatantly honest with yourself.

Combine these two brainstorming sessions, then brainstorm all of your possible business ideas. Research online for different businesses in some fields that you are interested in. What is every possible avenue, within a particular area that you could pursue? And which one is best in line with your values, skills and desires?

Once you have a general idea, work to clarify all aspects of the business. Think of all the products and/or services you want to sell and how you will sell them. Think of where your business could be located. What would it look like for you to open and run this business? How much time and effort will you devote to this? Would you have employees? Would you rent or own a space? Would you work from home? Who would your

1

customers be and how would you reach them? What would your day-to-day responsibilities be? Have you seen similar businesses? What did you like and dislike about them? Pretend you own this business presently and a stranger asks what you do; how would you respond?

Do not get discouraged if you are not yet able to answers these questions; you will gain insight and answers as you read further, but it is important to get into the habit of brainstorming and clarifying all of your ideas. Put them down on paper, add them into your phone, type them out in a computer document or use dictation to record them so that you can begin to develop an evolving list that will help guide many of your decisions. If you are unsure what you truly want to do or what would be the best fit for your lifestyle and values, check out the prequel to this book, *Seeds of an Entrepreneur*. *Seeds of an Entrepreneur* is a short book meant to accompany this book, full of advice and exercises to help you figure out your perfect fit.

# Chapter 2

# Business Myths De-Bunked

There are many factors that sway, either positively or negatively, people who want to start their own business. Factors including high financial potential, ability to work less and make your own schedule, and hopes of having less stress sound very appealing to many.

Although these are all possible, they are not all likely, at least at first. Depending on the business you start, you may make far less money than your current job, have to work more hours and have increased stress. It is important to evaluate your values and goals before starting this venture and picking your business model. Make sure that you start a business for the right reasons instead of being guided by misleading, false assumptions.

Just as potential components may allure some, many possible factors and myths prevent others from taking the leap. Take, for example, the myth that 80-90 percent of small business fail. The Bureau of Labor Statistics found that after two years the majority actually succeed and after 5 years half remain successful.

Another myth is that prosperous entrepreneurs are all "sharks" with MBAs and a keen business sense. There have been all kinds of people with different backgrounds and education, and various strengths and skills, who have succeeded in business. Becoming an entrepreneur is not a one-size-fits-all process. You have to be aware of your strengths, weaknesses, values and goals to set yourself up for your own personal success. The more education, planning and assistance you can get the more likely you will be to become part of the 50 percent who succeeds after five years.

Every industry is different and every entrepreneur is different. Research the industry you want to enter, and do not let misleading information influence your future business decisions. Become curious about everything you hear and read. Find out what makes certain businesses profitable and others failures. Learn from others but also utilize your own skills to shape your strategy and set yourself up for success.

# Chapter 3

## Market Research and Competitive Analysis: Who, What, When, Where, How?

Sam had an idea for a product. His friends and family told him it was great. He used his savings, borrowed money and got a small loan to start his business. He spent 6 months perfecting his idea. He spent a lot of money getting the perfect website, ad campaigns, logo design and packaging. He seemingly did everything right, yet he struggled to make sales. He continued to spend time and money on advertising, with little return on his investment. How could this have gone wrong when he had done everything right?

Sam did everything right, besides making sure people would pay for his product.

It does not matter what your website, store, packaging or logo looks like if you do not have customers interested in your business idea. Once you have an idea, market research and competitive analysis should be your next steps. Figure out who your customers are, what needs they have that are not being met, and the best way to reach them. This will determine how and where you set up, market and advertise your business. The better you know who your target demographic is, the better you can work to meet their needs.

Get clear and specific when developing your ideal demographic. For example, if you open a bar you are not just going to target adults who like to drink alcohol. You will need to decide age ranges, socioeconomic status, interests, hobbies, lifestyle, etc. A bar targeted towards college students looks much different than one targeted to young professionals. Before you start your business and develop a marketing plan, write down a detailed description of your target customer: Age and/or stage of life (i.e. parents of young children can be 22 or 42, but both are in the same stage), gender, geographic locations, race, religion, marital and family status, income, spending habits, hobbies, lifestyle, interests. A common strategy is to make up a "customer avatar", meaning a description of your one ideal customer for whom the rest of your planning will be geared towards. The rest of this chapter will illustrate strategies for finding this information.

An easy place to begin your research is online. Search on www.google.com/trends to help you determine what the life span, regional popularity and top search queries of a certain idea or product. Reference libraries are also a beneficial, underutilized resource. Ask the librarian to help you to find information about competition and demographics in your niches. They will be able to help you navigate online systems, with information about net profits of similar businesses, number of employees, etc., that are not available to the general public unless you pay. Both of these strategies will help you determine if there is a market for your idea and a broad understanding of who that market is.

Use your competitors to gain further insight into who your target market will be. Go to their physical location (if there is one) and spend some time observing their customers. Go to your competitors' websites and social media profiles. Look at who follows them on social media and who comments and likes their posts. If they have a blog, examine who comments on the blog and what they say. You can often tell who your competition is targeting based on the language they use and content they put out. The more competitive research you can do the better, so it will be helpful to keep track of everything using Excel or another type of spreadsheet.

Once you have a general idea of who your target market is, the next step is to get clear on their needs. There are several ways you can do this. People reveal a lot about themselves in the comment sections in blogs, YouTube videos, and online forums. Explore websites and forums where you think your target demographic may hang out, such as Quora ([www.quora.com](www.quora.com)) and Reddit ([www.reddit.com](www.reddit.com)), or niche specific forums.

For example, if you want to design yoga apparel simply type "yoga forum" into search engines and discover multiple results. When reading through these comments look for information about lifestyle: if they are single, have kids, where they work, where they live, what else they are interested in, and most important what they are struggling with and what needs are not being met. Perhaps you consistently see people complaining about their inability to find high quality, reasonably priced yoga clothes. These could be the customers you target with your products and marketing.

Gain invaluable insight by reading reviews of similar products or businesses. In these reviews people will reveal why they bought a product or visited a business, how they found out about it, how their needs were met and what needs were not met. Use all of this information to determine how you will meet the unmet needs of your demographic. You may have to shift who your target customer is after reading these. For example, you initially want to open a yoga studio targeted towards women aged 22-40, yet with more research you realize that there is a huge unmet need for studios in your area that provide classes of pregnant women and the older population. If you add prenatal yoga and geriatric yoga classes into your schedule you can draw unique customers whose needs are not being met by your competition. Be open to changing your initial ideas to best meet the needs of your future customers.

After having an idea of who your target customer is and how you will meet their needs, try to talk to people who you would target. Go to local establishments and talk to their customers or ask questions online about what people want. This may seem nerve wracking to some, but remember that you are not selling anything and people love the opportunity to talk about themselves.

Examine your competition not only to clarify your target market, but also to learn and prepare. How does your competition make money? Physical location, online or both? How big are they? Where are they located? How profitable are they? How do they market? How are their services and products priced? What is their mission statement? What is their tone-informal or formal? What is their focus (customer service, high quality products, inexpensive products)?

Gain as much information as you can to prepare how you will penetrate this market. What can you model after them and how will you differentiate yourself? Sign up to their email lists and follow them on social media to gain insight into how they reach their customers. Competition is not bad; it means that there is a need for the product or service, and the key is to meet this need in a new, unique way.

Learn your market well. How large is your market? How many competitors do you have? And realistically what percentage of this market can you capture?

# Chapter 4

## There's More Than One Way to Start a Business — What's Right for You?

There are many ways to start a business and there are pros and cons with each of them. The key is to find the one that has more pros than cons for your business idea. There are also different ways to set businesses up legally. This chapter will briefly go over each type of business but if you are interested in a certain one, research it in-depth before making any final decisions.

You will first need to decide who you will be selling to. Will you be selling to businesses (B2B) or customers (B2C)? If you plan to sell physical products think about the following: If you manufacture or import products you can sell to distributors or wholesalers who sell products to retailers or you can sell directly to customers. Will you be manufacturing or buying from a wholesaler or distributor? Where will you store your products? Will you manufacture be in the US or outside of the US? Will you sell on a platform, like Amazon, Etsy or Ebay?

All of these types of business models will have entirely different pricing and marketing strategies, as well as costs associated with them. Making a product from scratch and selling it directly to customers online will look very different than importing products from overseas and selling them to businesses.

The most common way to start a business is to open a new bricks and mortar business. This is a business that is started with your own concept and is placed in a physical location. Examples could be restaurants, boutiques, and service-based businesses with an office (lawyers, accountants, therapists). The advantage of this is you have 100% creative freedom and if you find the right location, you can have high traffic. The biggest downside is the overhead costs of starting and running this type of business. Rent, utilities, inventory, insurance, equipment are just a few of the costs. Also, you have to generate your own customers, unlike if you bought a business with an existing customer base.

A second choice for a bricks and mortar business is to buy an existing business or a franchise. With these, the name is known and you have an existing customer base. This could help of hinder your success, depending on the reputation of the business you bought. Also, be cautious of the existing business' debts and loans. Franchises will have fees, financial and asset requirements and ongoing royalties. You will have a very structured way to run the business but little freedom as an independent owner.

A popular option, because of the ease and low cost, is an online based business. There are plenty of tools making it easy for those who are not tech savvy to open and run various types of online businesses. The freedom and low cost are two draws to this type of business structure, but it comes with its own drawbacks as well. It is much harder to drive traffic, and conversion rates are much lower in online businesses than in bricks and mortar businesses. You have to spend a lot of time and money focusing on producing free content, such as blogging, or marketing on various online platforms to bring in customers. There will be a lot of competition that you may not have when opening a bricks and mortar location, as you are competing with everyone in you niche online. Also, working from home can become isolating and it can be hard to stay on track. There are, however, plenty of tactics to become successful online and it can be a great place to start and test an idea without spending a lot of money.

# Chapter 5

## Nuts and Bolts of Business Structures

Before you can open your business you will need to choose a legal business structure and understand the government regulations that affect your business. You will have to pick an entity and register your business, usually at the state level. The structure you choose will have legal and tax implications. The U.S. Small Business Administration website ([www.sba.org](www.sba.org)) is a good resource to read about different structures and their implications.

A common choice among small businesses is the LLC structure. Becoming an LLC, Limited Liability Company, is one of the more popular ways to structure a business because, as its name suggests, it provides limited liability features that protect personal assets. Obtaining an LLC varies by state, but it is usually is not a complicated process. There are lawyers who help set this up and there are online legal services that specialize in helping new businesses get started. Some entrepreneurs, however, feel confident to file for it without professional assistance. To find out more information, go to your state's Secretary of State website.

In addition, you have the option to start a business as a sole proprietor (one person owns and is personally liable), as a partnership (partners own and are held liable), as a "C" Corporation (protected from liability but are strictly regulated) or "S" Corporation (owners protected from liability and must comply with regulations). All businesses must be registered either by the state (LLC and Corporations) or county (Sole Proprietors). Liability and taxation varies for each of these options. It is highly suggested that you consult a lawyer and accountant to decide the best option for you.

After registering your business you will need to get a tax identification number, called an Employer Identification Number (EIN) for your business. You will need this to apply for a business banking account or credit cards as well as filing your taxes. You can do this for free at the IRS website.

# Chapter 6

# Professional Help — Lawyers, Accountants, Employees, Oh My!

It is unlikely and not recommended that you take care of everything yourself when running a business. The money you would pay a professional could save hours of your valuable time.

The first two professionals you will likely contact are a lawyer and an accountant. They can help you get everything set up. You will not need ongoing assistance from these professionals, at least in the beginning, but they will be there to help get you started and to provide services when needed (i.e., time to file taxes).

If you do not want to track your finances yourself you can also hire a bookkeeper, whose rate are much cheaper than an accountant, to handle them on a periodic basis. Another professional that will assist is an insurance agent to make sure that your business is fully covered. Talk with an agent to see what type of coverage you need: property, liability, workers comp, so on.

After you have gotten all of your professional help lined up, you can think of contracted help. This could be a graphic designer to design your logo, a web designer to set up your website, or any other person you will pay on a per project basis. If you are short on start-up funds you can find people online for much cheaper than you would expect, but the quality of work can vary. Websites like fivver, Upwork, and Freelancer all have contract employees ready to take on your next job.

Finally, decide if you are going to have employees, how many, and their roles, as this will affect your financial projections. You can get an idea from scoping out your competition. How many employees do they have in various roles during different days and times? If you work alone, you can decide if you want to hire a part-time or full-time administrative assistant or virtual assistant (an assistant who works from their home) to help with tasks such as email management, social media management, and other daily mundane tasks that take up your valuable time. Often these employees can do these tasks faster and better than you, and many entrepreneurs find it is worth the investment.

If you have employees you will need to decide how you will pay them. Will you handle payroll or hire a company? If you decide to handle it yourself, you must be very aware and stay up-to-date on the laws and taxes.

# Chapter 7

# Paying Uncle Sam

Taxes can be tricky and get a lot of business owners in trouble. This is why it is wise to talk to an accountant and possibly a financial advisor to know what you are required to pay.

Think of the last time you shopped for anything. You likely had to pay taxes on the goods you purchased. If you are selling goods you will need to collect those sales taxes, report them and pay them.

How you file your business and personal taxes will vary depending on how you structure your business. Keep track of all spending on your business to use as tax write-offs; again a professional can help guide you in this.

But remember that not all of the profit is yours to keep even if you put it back into your business, and a percentage of sales should be put aside to have sufficient funds to pay the IRS. Getting a clear understanding and developing a plan to have the right amount of money when Uncle Sam comes knocking will save you a lot of headaches, not to mention a potential IRS audit.

# Chapter 8

## Get Your Money Right — Funding and Finances

When you initially consider finances think of three separate components: start-up costs, overhead costs, and financial resources. Inadequate capital is the number one factor in failing businesses. Set yourself up for success by planning ahead! If you go to www.score.org you can get free financial planning worksheets to help organize the information listed below. (You will need to provide an email address to get access, but this is a non-profit organization and will not try to sell anything to you.)

Start-up costs is the amount of money that you will need to open-your doors (literally or figuratively). If you plan to get funding you will need to figure this out in detail, but even those who plan to fund their business themselves should also make a detailed list of start-up costs. If you are starting a bricks and mortar business, think of initial purchase or leasing costs of buildings and any construction or remodeling that needs done. For any business, think of equipment costs, including furniture, machinery, computer, and office supplies. Do you need to purchase materials, inventory or shipping supplies?

Next think of administrative costs, such as fees, permits or taxes, real estate and utility deposits, professional fees (legal, accounting, contractors, etc.), insurance, salaries/payroll taxes/payroll services/benefits, any online management or social media management.

Finally, figure out your advertising and promotional expenses, such as developing a website, email service provider, online and/or physical advertisements, signage and logo design, business cards or any other printed materials, travel expenses, or any other promotional items you need to purchase (i.e. promo gifts, table and canopy for events, etc.). Think of any other possible expense you might need to start. Begin by brainstorming in each of these categories and writing down everything you think you will need. Then do research on the costs associated with each item. Always over-estimate and plan to spend more than initially planned.

Repeat this process to figure out your monthly expenses. What will you need to pay for rent, utilities, phone and internet, insurance, professional fees (accounting, legal, bookkeeping, payroll), salaries, contracted employees (social media management, graphic designer, etc.), operating supplies (office supplies), monthly subscriptions to email service, bookkeeping service, website, etc., advertising, taxes, loan payments and interest, repairs or maintenance, travel, and any other monthly expenses that apply to your business? Note: If this business will be your fulltime job, remember to incorporate your salary into these monthly expenses.

Now take the start-up costs and at least the first three months of monthly expenses to get a figure of how much money you will need to start. Most businesses are not profitable initially and need extra cushion to cover the costs until they are making money to prevent them from going into the hole immediately.

After you get your business registered and obtain an EIN (the tax number given to your business), get a business banking account and credit card. A bookkeeping system such as Quickbooks or Xero will help you easily keep track of all expenses. You can connect your business accounts to this system for easy tracking. You can also track using an excel file. Every month you will need to track your Profits and Losses. These numbers will help you become clear on where your businesses stands financially. You can also track trends and analyze what marketing and selling strategies worked and which ones did not.

For example, if you spent 100 dollars on an advertising campaign and saw your profits increase by 2000 dollars, you likely would want to replicate that advertising strategy again to see if you get similar results. Only numbers will be able to give you this concrete data.

A stress-inducing question is how you will get the money to pay for your business idea, now that you know how much you will need. Some business advisors advise against borrowing money. When you borrow, a lot of your profits go towards paying off the loan and you can be pressured to run your business a certain way to be profitable instead of taking risks. If you do not want to borrow money, think of how you can start small and build rather than immediately embarking on a high cost venture. If you can demonstrate success on a small level, it will show favorably to banks and investors if and when you decide to apply for additional funding later on. It is not a bad idea to start small to test out your market before investing a large amount of money.

Many businesses have started because of loans or investors. Applying for a business loan or reaching out to investors can be nerve-wracking and, unfortunately, many do not get approved. You absolutely must be prepared, know your numbers and have a concrete, feasible plan. Lenders look for good credit, expertise and commitment (why it is often a good idea to start small to prove this), a detailed business plan, adequate equity and collateral. Lenders will want to know that your company will be able to repay the amount borrowed, when you will begin to be profitable, how much of a profit and if the profit can be sustained. They also look at your personal investment in the business and any tangible items used for collateral. All loans will have terms and conditions, such as its intended purpose, the amount and the length.

Another option is crowdfunding, which is the practice of obtaining small amounts of funding from a large amount of people. There are platforms online, such as Kickstarter, where billions of dollars have been raised for businesses and other causes. You can put a picture, a video and a story of your business and the general public can donate any amount of money to you. You can also offer incentives for different amounts of donations.

For example, if you are starting a restaurant you can offer a free appetizer for anyone who donates 20 dollars or more. It is a great starting point and can help get the word out about your product or idea. People who invested will also likely be future customers. Because of the gain in popularity, some platforms have become saturated but if you can get friends and family to help share via social media or word of mouth, you have the potential to raise a lot of money.

Using personal loans and financing (friends and family, personal savings, home equity loan) is another route that some take. This can be a good option as business loans can be very difficult to obtain, but only if you have a concrete plan in place. Just because you are not applying for a business loan does not mean that you should not have a detailed plan of how you will be able to pay back the money. The mistake some run into is they take out these loans without a plan and they go into personal debt or put friends and family into debt because of their inability to pay back the loan in an allotted time frame.

There are entire books on funding and financing. Deciding the best plan for you will take some further research and it is common to have several plans, such as using personal savings and crowdfunding, followed by applying for a loan.

# Chapter 9

# Profits and Pricing

There are many factors that contribute to how you price your items and services. Take some time to do research before deciding on your pricing. You can always change your prices later on, but make sure that you do not initially price items too high or too low. If you start too low you will likely lose customers when you try to raise them and if you start too high it will prevent many interested customers from buying. Use the previous customer and competition research to help determine your pricing strategy. Who are your customers: salary, spending habits, life stage? How much money are they willing to spend on particular products and services? How is your competition pricing their products or services and what do they offer in return?

Let's look at various ways you can price your products/services based on how your competition prices them:

Your competitors price similar products between 55-85 dollars. Let's look at how you can price your items to get a sales revenue of 5000.

If you priced yours at 55 dollars, you would make 5000 with 90 paying customers.

If you priced yours at 65 dollars, you would make 5000 with 77 paying customers.

If you priced yours at 75 dollars, you would make 5000 with 67 paying customers.

If you priced yours at 85 dollars, you would make 5000 with 59 paying customers.

As you can see, the lower you price your items, the more customers you will need. Do you plan to get more customers than your higher priced competition? How? Or do you plan to charge higher prices than your lower priced competition? If so, how will you convince those customers to pay more?

Furthermore, think if you will have one product or service or multiple. When selling various products, or a mixed demo, find out what makes you the most money and mix that with products with the highest mark-up. What are people coming to you for? And what can you add to this to make additional profits? Upselling and cross-selling can drastically increase your revenue. Train employees to offer additional products or services, physically place like items together and use signage to encourage an upsell. Offer a discount (buy one get one 50% off) or bundle products at a discounted price. If you run an online business, add an upsell offer after they put a similar item in the cart, or have similar items listed on an item page ("Customers who bought this also bought that").

Additionally, strategize ways to get return customers, those who have bought from you before, to buy again. You can use loyalty programs, discounts offered through email marketing, and offer products or services they will need to return for. If your product or service is something that people need once in a lifetime then you will focus all of you time and money trying to get new customers. If you offer products or services people will return to you to get, your initial goal will be new customer acquisition but as your business grows, much of your efforts will be geared towards return customers. Someone who has purchased from you before is more likely than a new potential customer to purchase again. Knowing this information will help you plan and target your marketing efforts.

Now let's get into some pricing strategy. Profit is king. It is how you will keep your business alive and be able to make a comfortable living for yourself. When considering pricing strategies examine if will you make a profit with that strategy. You need to first know your Break Even Analysis, which is simply how much money you need to make to cover your costs (everything discussed in previous chapter, rent, salaries, supplies, etc.). There will be fixed costs, those that stay constant (rent, insurance, utilities), that are paid no matter what, and variable costs, those that fluctuate based on a company's production (inventory, supplies). Variable Costs go up as a company produces more good or services and goes down as company produces less good or services.

A bakery will always have to pay the same amount of rent, insurance, and equipment rental costs (fixed), but will need to spend more or less on sugar, flour and butter, depending on how many baked goods they produce each month (variable). Based on these number, you can then decide what pricing strategy would work best for you. Knowing both of these numbers will allow you to know how profitable you will be if you produce more or less.

There are several financial terms that are frequently used in business. Knowing what they mean will be helpful anytime you are reading about finances or just in communication with professionals in the business field. It will also help to make sense of you own financial planning. These terms are broken down below:

*Sales Revenue* = Price x Units Sold (This is TOTAL amount of money brought in)

Example: You sold 10 T-Shirts priced at 20 dollars. Sale Revenue is 200 dollars.

*Gross Profit* = Sales Revenue – Variable Costs

Example: The T-Shirts cost 5 dollars per shirt (50 dollars total) to make and package. Gross Profit for the 10 T-shirts sold is 150 dollars.

*Net Profit* = Gross Profit – Fixed Costs

Example: During the time it took to sell those 10 T-Shirts, you spent 50 dollars paying employees, and in rent and utilities (fixed costs). Your Net Profit 100 dollars.

The total money your business brought in was 200 but after accounting for variable costs and fixed costs, the actual profit was 100 dollars. This is the strategy you can use to figure out how much profit your business is actually making.

To determine your pricing strategy, think in terms of your Gross Margin. Gross Margin is the amount of profit you make. It is the difference between Revenue (Cost Sold) and Cost of Goods and is expressed as a percentage. For example, if a product in your company is sold at 1000 dollars and the cost of goods are 750, the calculation would be:

1000-750/1000

250/1000

25%

After you figure out what your Break Even Analysis (how much you need to make to cover all costs) is and your Gross Margin, you can begin to calculate the number of sales/paying customers you will need each day to cover your costs. Let's look at a few example:

*Example 1:*

Average Cost of Purchase: 12 dollars (How much the average paying customer spends)

Gross Margin: 50%

Open Days Per Month: 20

Break Even Analysis: 10,000/month. Need to make $500/day to cover all costs.

12 x .50=6 (6 dollars is the amount of money you make on each 12 dollar purchase)

500/6=83 sales per day. You need 83 paying customers to break even.

*Example 2:*

Average Cost of Purchase: 15 dollars

Gross Margin: 50%

Open Days/Month: 20

Break Even Analysis: 10,000/month. Need to make $500/day.

15 x .50=7.50

500/7.5=67 sales per day. You need 67 paying customers to break even if your average purchase increases to 15 dollars.

*Example 3:*

Average Cost of Purchase: 15 dollars

Gross Margin: 70%

Open Days/Month: 20

Break Even Analysis: 10,000/month. Need to make $500/day.

15 x .70=10.50

500/10.50=48 sales per day. You need 48 paying customers to break even if your average purchase is raised to 15 dollars and your gross margin is increased to 70%.

You have many options to help increase profits, such as keeping fixed costs low, increasing gross margin, increase sales per transaction and increasing number of paying customers. As you can see, you need fewer customers if you have higher profit margins but will need more customers if you keep your profits low. These prices will determine both your marketing and selling strategies.

# Chapter 10

## If You Build It They Will Come (Or They Won't) — Marketing Your Business

Starting the business is the easy part. The hard part is driving customers to your business and converting these customers into paying customers. Your marketing strategy will vary depending on who your ideal customers are. Keep in mind that people need to build trust in your brand and company before they give you their money. The way you market and run your business will either facilitate this trust or drive people away.

Take some time now to think of how your favorite businesses advertise. What turned you into a loyal customer? How did you first hear about them?

Have you come across advertisements that seemed off-putting? Why?

Are there businesses that you won't go to? Why?

You can ask friends and family the same questions to get insights into what people like and dislike about businesses and marketing. This can help you to start generating your own ideas. Keep those ideas in mind as we discuss some of the main strategies to spread the word about your business.

The oldest marketing tactic is word-of-mouth. Are you more likely to try a new restaurant after a trusted friend recommends it? Have you ever liked something a friend had and asked where he/she had gotten it? This is easy marketing for those businesses. In a world of social media, internet blogs, and online reviews, word of mouth has drastically grown. Studies have shown that reviews on a business or product greatly determine if a customer chooses to go there or buy the product.

But how can you gain this reputation when you are first starting? There are several ways. The first is to reach out to blogs, papers or influencers in your niche or a related niche. For example, if you just opened a bakery you may reach out to wedding planners and offer free cake samples. Do not ask for anything in return, and expect that you will be ignored some of the time. All you need is that one wedding planner to agree, love your samples and spread the word.

Offer free products to blog writers or social media influencers. They may or may not write about your product, but again all you need is one article to get the ball rolling.

Often local newspapers and social media accounts will post stories about new businesses. Reach out to them and let them know you would love to be featured. It is also a great idea to offer discounts or coupons to followers of these writers.

Another tactic to encourage word-of-mouth marketing is to implement a referral program, in which people get discounts when they refer a friend. This might take some work and a little money in the beginning but word of mouth will be a constant, free source of traffic to your business if implemented correctly.

Physical advertisements, in the form of signs, flyers, or post cards are often used by bricks and mortar businesses. The most important advertisement is your signage. People need to be able to see you are there and have an idea of the type of business you run. There is a business in my neighborhood that I pass every day. The sign is dark and hard to read, the name is ambiguous and the windows are always shut. After a year of driving past it, they had the windows open and I saw it was a hair salon. If I would have known, I would gone there when I first moved to the neighborhood. Now, it can be the best salon in the city, but I will never go there, just because the appearance is so off-putting. Do not let something that simple ruin your success. A new business opened, right next door to this mysterious salon, that had a clear sign indicating it offered a workout service and handed out cards for a free class. It was packed during opening week, and handing people physical advertisements, that offered an incentive, drove a lot of business.

When thinking of your own advertising strategy, consider places where your customers would go and see if you can put up flyers or offer the workers some coupons to give out. Also look up any events that you can have a table and hand out cards, coupons, or free gifts (like pens or koozies with your company's information on them) to help spread the word.

Even if you plan to open a physical location, it would be very wise to also advertise on an online platform. When you want to find a new place, what do you typically do? I would guess that the majority of answers are "Google it". Search engines account for over 60 percent of website traffic, with Google being the largest driver and Bing coming in second.

Type in anything to a search engine and see how many results come up. If you simply type in 'bars' almost 1 billion results are found, yet only 10 or so are featured on the first page. The businesses on that first page have put in work, either time, money, or both. You can register your business in Google making it easier for local visitors to find it when they are searching (i.e. Coffee Shop locations in Orlando FL). It is difficult, however, to make your website to show up in a search. The term SEO, Search Engine Optimization, is used to describe ways to make your website visible in search engines. There are many ways to increase your SEO ranking (where you show up on search engine results pages). You can pay for assistance or try to do it organically. Beware of any services that claims to get your website on the first page of a search engine immediately. They use "Black Hat" techniques, which means they temporarily scam the system and your website can face some serious penalties when the search engine finds out.

Email marketing is a marketing technique used by almost all successful businesses. In the online world, platforms are constantly changing. Google frequently makes changes to its algorithm, meaning how it decides what websites rank high on searches. Also Facebook made a change so that many posts by businesses pages are not seen by its followers and now Instagram is implementing some changes.

The only thing that does not change is email. You own your emails and nobody can take them away. The obstacle in email marketing is you have to make sure your recipients see and open the emails. Think of when and how you scroll through your emails. The increased use of smart phones has drastically changed how we look at emails. We often browse while we are waiting for something, a friend to arrive, waiting in line, possibly at a stop light. When you do this, which emails do you typically open? Most likely important ones and those that jump out. There are many tactics that you can implement to use emails to market and make your "open-rates" higher.

You will need an email service to send out mass emails. It doesn't look professional to send them out from a personal account and you will not be able to send mass emails this way. Many start out with MailChimp, as it is free up to a certain amount of subscribers, but there are plenty of email providers out there that will meet the needs of your business.

The final form of online marketing is Social Media Marketing. This has become very popular as it is easy and free to start and run social media accounts for your business. There are also ads that you can buy on many of the platforms that allow you to specifically target your audience. There are a lot of social media platforms to choose from, including Facebook, Twitter, Instagram, Pinterest, Periscope, Snapchat, Google+, LinkedIn, and Tumbler, along with forums, such as Quora and Reddit, that you can participate in.

With all of the options, it is best to start with one or two, grow these, and then decide if you want to expand to other platforms. Think of what you are selling and where your audience is hanging out. If you are selling beautiful jewelry, then visual sites like Instagram and Pinterest will likely be profitable platforms. If you are selling information-based products or services, then Facebook, Twitter or LinkedIn may be a great starting point.

When researching your competition, look into all of their social media accounts and find the ones that they are having the most success and engagement (followers, comments, likes), and select from these platforms to start. When doing social media marketing, make sure that the majority of your content is non-promotional. The 80/20 rule is what many follow, meaning that 80 percent is good, valuable content, and 20 percent is promotion for your business. If you do it right, that 20 percent will drive you far more traffic and sales than if you only advertised.

# Chapter 11

## Why Branding is Much More Than Your Logo

When asked what a brand is, many answer by saying the company's logo or catch phrase. Although this is part of the brand, it is just a small part. Think about popular logos, such as the McDonalds "M" or the Starbucks mermaid. What comes to mind when you think of these images? The thoughts will be different for everyone, but most likely it elicits some thoughts and emotions. Perhaps you thought how much you loved certain products or were reminded of a negative experience you had. Use this to shape your brand. What will others think when they are asked to picture your logo?

Although you have no control over the thoughts or reactions of others, you can have a goal of what you want your business to represent to your customers. Keep this in mind anytime you think about branding, naming your business, designing your logo, or deciding on you mission statement.

The following questions will you develop your brand:

What is the reason customers should listen and trust you? How will your company gain this trust?

Who is your ideal customer? How can you reach them?

What can you promise them that your competition cannot? What do you want your customers to feel when they think of your business?

Once you have brainstormed answers to the above questions you can begin to plan how you will communicate your brand message to your ideal customers. The clearer you can convey the message of how your business is relevant to your customers and is better than your competitors, the more successful your brand will become.

There are four "P's" in branding that you will need to answer for yourself and to your customer:

1. Purpose: Why does your company exist? Customers love to hear about your story, and "About Us" pages on websites are frequently visited before purchasing. Be as authentic as you can and your ideal customers will begin to relate. Think of where you are headed in the future.

2. Promise: What can you promise them that others cannot? Do not make promises you cannot keep as this is a fast way to lose customer loyalty. Pick one or two main promises. This will make you seem genuine and memorable.

3. Personality: What is the culture of your company? Is it fun and lighted hearted or serious? Is it open to everyone or exclusive? This can be expressed in all areas of your business, from customer service, to language and style of emails or product descriptions. How do you plan to express this?

4. Positioning: How are you positioned in the market and against your competitors? How can you sway others to turn to you instead of a company they have trusted for years? What needs are you meeting? How are you unique and how can you convey this to your target customers? Perhaps your competitors are notorious for poor customer service; then your positioning might be guaranteed customer service.

The most important part to remember about branding is that it is meant to help your customers, not you. It is as if your customer is an actor and you are their agent, getting them the roles that they want. The customer is the star and you help them to stardom. So make sure that you are meeting the needs of others and not just yourself.

Next, think of how you can share your message to the right people. Branding will drive your marketing strategies as well as your management strategies. The clearer you are in what your brand represents, the easier it will be to make various business decisions.

# Chapter 12

## Business Plans Made Simple

If you have searched online for business startup advice, most likely you have read about business plans. These can seem overwhelming and daunting and even deter some from starting.

The information in this book has addressed most of the aspects incorporated in business plans. It consists of an executing summary of your business (which should be done last), narratives on business aspects, financial forecasts, and supporting data. The website www.score.org has a free business plan template as well as financial planning worksheets. As mentioned earlier, it is non-profit and completely free, but you will need to provide an email to get access to the resources. There are many different websites that also provide templates that you can plug in your information, making business plan far less daunting. Let's quickly go over the components of each section:

In the *Business Section*, you will provide information including a business description, description of your products and services, the market need for your products and services, your location and why you selected it, an assessment of you competition and how you will beat them, a description of your personal experience and background and how this benefits your company as well as any other management personnel's background and characteristics, and how you will use the funds (if you are asking for them).

In the *Financial Forecast*, you will provide a capital equipment list, projected income and expenses, assets, liabilities and equity, sources and uses of funds (cash flow), and your break-even analysis.

In the *Supporting Data Section*, you will show that you have done your research by providing backup information for all of your claims. You will need to provide facts and where you got this information.

Business plans are vital for obtaining funding but the true value lies within all of the research and thought that goes into making one. It may take a while, but the process of systematically thinking through all aspects of your business protects you from making costly, devastating mistakes in the future. You may find that your original plan changes quite a bit through this process, which is a good thing. It is better to make changes prior to investing tons of your valuable time and finances. Even if you do not plan to get loans or funding, a business plan will be your biggest investment to ensure success. Do not skip this step, even if it seems overwhelming at first.

# Conclusion

Congrats on completing this basic business book. The intent of this book is to give you very basic knowledge and introduce you to concepts involved in starting your own business. It is perfectly normal to feel overwhelmed as it is a lot of new information. The more you learn, the less overwhelming the information becomes. To prevent potential burnout, focus on just one thing at a time. Don't worry about email marketing when you are figuring out your business structure. Each little step you take will bring you one step closer to opening your dream business and changing your life. Keep this in mind and good luck!

Finally if you enjoyed this book, please be sure to leave a review and a comment to let me know how I can continue to bring you quality books. I sincerely appreciate you reading and reviewing Startup Essentials!

# About the Author

I sat on the trolley every morning and evening commuting to and from work. To a job that required a Master's degree. A job that took six years in school with a 4.0 GPA and six months after graduating with my M.A. to get. A job that I moved and bought a house for and was very excited to begin. A job that quickly sucked the life out of me, yet I continued to work at for over four years. So, for over four years, I sat on that trolley and looked at the fellow commuters. They all looked miserable. I would sit there every day thinking *I do not want to be riding on this trolley for the remainder of my working years.* Nevertheless, I sat there year after year and never made a change. Often my co-worker and I would talk about the businesses we would want to open and how fun it would be to live a life other than one where we dreaded work each day. It always seemed like a nice dream to fantasize about but one that never seemed in reach. I remember telling my supervisor in grad school I just wanted a job I looked forward to working each day and she scoffed at the seemingly naïve comment. It seemed I always had this feeling there was more out there but I did not know what it was.

It was not until I moved to a new city that a shift began. I moved for a new, happy life but soon fell back into old routines, applying for jobs I was not passionate about for salaries far beneath what I wanted. A simple discussion with my boyfriend, in which he stated there should be more pet stores in our dog-friendly area, prompted my mind shift. I love animals. I had money from selling my house and I could be the one to open this pet store!

I began to explore opening a bricks and mortar pet boutique. The neighborhood I lived in was full of dogs and I was confident it would be a success. I went to the library and started to search for books about business. They all seemed so boring and dry, until I found one that drew me in. Through reading this book, I learned that people from all walks of life, with different passions, have been successful opening their own businesses. This gave me a boost of confidence.

I found a local non-profit that offered business classes for those interested in starting their own businesses (www.score.org). I went through a 6 week course and was excited about continuing on this journey. To get experience in management, I became a manager at a coffee shop and also a dog walker while I continued to plan and look for store locations. I found out quickly, that I did not like managing. I was always on call. I remember taking a weekend trip and getting 5 calls on the way up from employees. This made me begin to question what it would be like if I opened up my own place. It made me a little uneasy to think about not having the freedom to enjoy a weekend away when I wanted. While this was happening, I was also not having any luck finding a location for a store in my area. In talking with my business mentor, I decided it would be a good idea to look into starting an online store while I continued to look for locations. I began to research this a bit further and realized it would be feasible. I had to, however, make an entirely new business plan. I began this process planning for a physical location but online was a new beast.

My online pet boutique was up and running within a few months of me making this decision. It is not initially easy to drive traffic to an online business but I began to see the potential of having a business based online. There was freedom in this. I could work from anywhere and make my own schedule. Every single day, I read tons of information, watched YouTube videos instead of TV, and listened to business podcasts in the car, instead of the radio. I also began a personal journey that involved intense work on my anxieties and mindset. I learned about manifesting and subconscious reprogramming, and applied the techniques. I became very honest with myself about what I truly wanted, and what personal traits and thoughts were holding me back from this. In the course of a year, I completely transformed.

I loved to tell my friends and family all the things I was learning and applying. I had some hiccups with my online pet boutique, due to manufacturer issues, and during this time re-evaluated what I truly wanted to do. Selling adorable animal products is fun but I wanted something more. Many online entrepreneurs have several businesses and I began to ponder what I could do next. I kept hearing about people fulfilling their "life purpose" and contemplated what that would look like for me. With my background in Psychology and Counseling, I felt compelled to help others. What a waste it would be for me to spend hours every day learning and developing all of these business and self-improvement techniques and not share them with anyone. Then I received a sign.

I was doing dishes, binge watching YouTube videos, when a video came on about writing and publishing books. I have always loved to write. As I sat down and watched the video and I was filled with excitement. I then searched for more free information online. I found Facebook groups where I learned from others doing this. I purchased several courses before beginning on this adventure. Everything about it just felt *right*. I can help others, use my formal background and education in Psychology, all my experience in starting and running a business, and do something I felt passionate about.

I understand that becoming an entrepreneur is about overcoming internal barriers as much as it is overcoming external barriers. My goal is to teach others how to overcome both. I share this long journey of mine to let you know it is not always a simple and straight road to success, but with the right tools and mindset you can get there. I hope to provide much more information with you on your road to success. Please reach out by signing up to my email list and shooting me a message about your current situation, triumphs, and struggles

# References:

Garzon, Juan. "Building a Brand People Love". Charlotte, NC. 14 February 2016. SCORE Power Lunch Series, Seminar.

The Score Foundation. (2014). Simple Steps for Starting your Business.

U.S. Small Business Administration. Choose Your Business Structure. Retrieved from https://www.sba.gov/starting-business/choose-your-business-structure.

55514893R00031

Made in the USA
Middletown, DE
10 December 2017